Media Studies

Contents

Introduction

About this guide 4

The A2 specification 5

Examinable skills 5

The examination 6

Organising your research 7

Research methodology 9

■ ■ ■

Content Guidance

About this section 12

Women and film 13

Popular music and youth culture 16

Politics and the media 19

Children and television 24

Sport and the media 30

Concept to consumption 32

Community radio 35

Audience research 37

Crime and the media 40

■ ■ ■

Questions and Answers

About this section 46

Topic 1: Women and film 47

Topic 2: Popular music and youth culture 52

Topic 3: Children and television 55

Topic 4: Sport and the media 59

Introduction

About this guide

This unit guide is for students following the OCR A2 Media Studies course. It deals with Unit 2734, the Critical Research Study, which is designed to assess your ability to carry out independent research, investigation and analysis of a media topic and to evaluate your findings. There are three sections:

- **Introduction** — this provides advice on how to use the guide, an explanation of the skills required for the Critical Research exam, an outline of the exam structure, guidance on organising your research, suggestions for research methodology and revision strategies.
- **Content Guidance** — this includes an outline of the areas open for investigation and specific guidance on how to approach research in each of these areas. It is designed to help you structure your preparation and make you aware of the content knowledge you should have for the exam.
- **Questions and Answers** — this provides sample questions and answers for the Critical Research exam. Some of the answers are of A-grade standard and others are C-grade responses. Examiner's comments are included to explain how the marks are awarded.

How to use the guide

To gain maximum benefit from this guide, use it systematically. Read through the Introduction carefully, taking note of the examinable skills, exam structure and tips on research and revision. When you have a thorough overview of the skills needed and the format of the exam, you will be ready to move on to the Content Guidance section.

The Content Guidance section leads you through the essential content areas you need to know for the exam, and highlights particular issues and debates. Make notes on your own examples and experiences as you read through this section to supplement the information you have gained in lessons.

When you have completed your study of content, you should move on to the Question and Answer section which gives examples of exam questions with A–grade or C–grade answers. Take note of the structure of the best answers, as well as the information they contain. You have a limited time in the exam, and part of your revision period should be used to practise writing comprehensive answers in timed conditions. Make sure that you read the examiner's comments on each answer, and note which features are praised and which are problematic.

Learning Centre / Canolfan Dysgu
Aberdare Campus
Tel: 01685 887510

The A2 specification

Unit 2734 brings together all of the skills of media analysis you have gained throughout your course. The knowledge and understanding of media products and institutions you have acquired, plus the insight into production issues gained through your practical work and the critical skills you have developed through the analysis of texts, will all be relevant to this exam. Your AS coursework and examinations, alongside the understanding of the media which you have gained through your A2 studies, will be invaluable.

In this unit you are required to conduct independent research on one media topic from the list below. The focus is on active investigation, concentrating on audience and institutional issues. The specification requires that you also consider academic and popular critical perspectives in the development of your own critical response.

The topics you can choose from are:
- women and film
- popular music and youth culture
- politics and the media
- children and television
- sport and the media
- concept to consumption
- community radio
- audience research (to be phased out after June 2004)
- crime and the media

Examinable skills

The main skill which the Critical Research Study assesses is your ability to carry out a thorough piece of independent research. Your goal is to create an appropriate research title, investigate your chosen topic in detail, and then present your findings in a systematic, substantiated and considered manner. You will have to answer two exam questions, each requiring different skills.

Question 1: research

You must produce evidence that you can:
- use a wide and appropriate range of primary sources (interviews and question-naires, films, television and radio programmes, newspapers, websites) and secondary sources (texts offering critical commentary on your chosen topic area)
- select appropriate resources from those available and discriminate between relevant and irrelevant information
- reference resources thoroughly and accurately and make points that are clear, relevant and have accurate substantiation

A2 Media Studies

- take control of the investigative process and not seem to be following any pre-existing research
- be reflective and evaluative of information obtained

Question 2: analysis and presentation

You must produce evidence that you can:
- create a clear, fluent and sophisticated argument, which is thoroughly substantiated and relates findings confidently to the wider topic
- use academic criticism and theoretical concepts with confidence and relate these to your own research findings
- create an original and discriminating response to your question, demonstrating an independent thought process behind your research
- use all investigative findings (from both your primary and secondary research) to inform your conclusions

The examination

The Critical Research Study exam is a 2-hour written examination worth 15% of the A2 grade. Within the 2 hours, you must answer two questions based on your own independent research. The questions are generic, which means that they can be applied to any of the topic areas.

Unit 2734 is slightly different from other Media Studies exams in that you are allowed to take four A4 sides of notes into the examination which must be submitted with your exam script. These notes, based on the research you have completed during the course of the unit, are an invaluable reference. They must be hand-written and must not include paragraphs, full sentences or detailed essay plans. If prepared properly, these notes can include all of the information you need to create a thorough exam answer.

Below is a checklist of the elements you should include in your notes:
- **(1)** A list of the primary sources (interviews, questionnaires, your own analyses of media texts) you used, research that you undertook and comments on the information you gained from this research. This should include any statistics or other data which might be relevant in the exam.
- **(2)** A list of all of the secondary sources (popular and academic criticism) which you used, including titles, authors, publication dates (and, for articles, the names of the journals in which they appeared). If your secondary sources include websites, you need to include the full web addresses. You should make evaluative notes on these secondary sources, stating how useful they were and how they related to the findings from your primary research.
- **(3)** A list of quotations which you think might be relevant to your exam answers, with full details of their sources.
- **(4)** Your reasons for choosing your topic of study and creating your focus question.

(5) Some consideration of the profiles, expectations and reactions of the audiences for texts within your study.

(6) A discussion of any institutional questions or considerations relating to your chosen topic.

(7) Notes on historical and social contexts as factors which may have had an influence on the area you are studying.

(8) Comments on your overall findings and how your primary and secondary research helped you come to these conclusions. Remember, there is nothing wrong with finding that you could come to no conclusions. It is the research process which is being examined, not your ability to find specific answers.

The first question on the Critical Research Study paper focuses on the *research* you have undertaken for your particular topic area. You are asked to give an account of your methods of research, commenting on both the primary and secondary research you undertook. In order to gain the highest possible marks in this section of the exam, you must make sure that you have commented on how you researched institutional issues, academic criticism, popular criticism and relevant issues concerning audience reception. Remember that your own consumption of media texts related to your topic is relevant here.

The second question in the exam asks you to *analyse and present* your findings. This is the section in which you can explain how you created your research question and how you came to your conclusions. You should discuss how both the primary and secondary research that you completed helped you to arrive at a particular critical interpretation of your topic.

Organising your research

As with any A-level research project, organisation is critical. If your notes are ordered properly from the outset, you can avoid the problems that occur when you attempt to revise from incomplete and disorganised notes. In order to ensure that the notes you take into the exam can be collated easily, you need to organise your research notes in a way that makes selecting the appropriate information a straightforward process. An effective method of organising your research notes is to create sections within a ringbinder folder which correspond to the sections of notes you will use in your four A4 sides of notes. Suggestions for these sections, and what to include in them, are given below.

Your topic of study and your focus question

These notes can be brief, but should explain why you selected your focus topic. You could consider how your own experiences might have affected your choice, whether your Media Studies course so far was influential, or whether you were drawn to the topic because of the lack of studies connected with it. In terms of the question itself, you should note what kind of debate it contains. Is your focus institutional, representational, context-related, audience-centred or connected to a particular conflict or controversy?

Primary research

What methods did you use in your primary research? Did you conduct interviews? If so, how did you come up with your questions? What kinds of questions did you use? Who did you interview and why did you choose those people? Where were the interviews conducted? Did you video, tape-record or make notes during the interviews? How did the place of the interview and the manner in which it was conducted affect the interview itself? If you used a focus-group approach, how did the participants in the research react to one another? If your research method included questionnaires, how did you decide on which questions to use? Were these open or closed questions? Who did you ask to complete the questionnaire and why?

Whether you chose to use interviews, focus groups or questionnaires, you should make detailed notes concerning your findings and how they helped you come to your conclusions. Your primary research might also include your own textual analysis of a film, newspaper, radio or television programme or other media text. You need to make notes not only on your analysis, but also on how it relates to any established critical opinion.

Secondary research

This section of your folder should include notes on both academic and popular criticism related to your chosen topic. You must record publication titles, authors, dates and publishers carefully in order to make accurate reference to your sources in the exam. Examiners look for a good range of sources, so if your initial list contains only websites, try to find books, magazines, newspapers and television documentaries which you can use. Note any quotations which you think would be useful in the exam, with accurate details of who said each one, when and in which kind of media text. A note on your own response to the ideas presented in your secondary sources is also important. Your exam answer should include comments on sources which you agreed and disagreed with, found useful and not so useful.

It is the process of research which is of particular interest to the examiner, and the strategies you use to collect your secondary materials should be commented on in the exam. Efficient collection of resources and materials ensures a thoroughly researched project. Use search engines on the internet to research information and make sure that you enter specific topics into the search engine. If you type 'children and television' into a search engine you will be faced with thousands of potential websites, most of which will be irrelevant to your focus question. If you type in 'children's game shows' the results are likely to be much more useful. The same applies to collecting print-based sources. Use library databases and book or magazine indexes to help you focus and refine your research.

Audience research

Your primary and secondary research notes should already contain comments on audience responses to any texts or organisations which are relevant to your chosen topic, but it is useful to include a separate section which relates solely to audience. What is the age, gender, race, religion or cultural profile of the audiences related to your texts or institutions? What expectations do the audiences have and do you think these expectations are fulfilled? In what contexts do audience members consume texts or relate to institutions and how does this affect their response?

Institutional detail

This section of your notes should detail the companies and organisations that are significant to your research area. What impact do these companies or organisations have on the media marketplace and the audiences they target? Have the companies or organisations you are considering undergone any recent changes or developments? What is their relationship with relevant legislation or new media technologies?

Context

In this section you should consider the impact of historical and social contexts on the topic you have chosen. Are there historical events which have affected your chosen research area? The impact of a war, for example, needs to be acknowledged if you have chosen to consider a question on politics and the media. Have changes in dominant social attitudes, expectations or habits affected your topic? Society's current appetite for cutting-edge technologies might, for example, be a relevant area to comment on if considering the presentation of sport in the media.

Your conclusions

This section does not need to be limited to your final thoughts. It is good practice to note down your responses to your question as you are in the process of investigation. In this way, you will be able to track the development of your ideas and will be able to comment fully in the exam on the processes by which you came to your final conclusions. If your ideas change during the course of your research, the examiner will be interested in the reasons why.

Research methodology

There are many complex models of research methodology, but there is no need to become confused by complicated research procedures. You will be using methodology properly if you follow a systematic plan of organisation such as the one outlined above. Part of your primary research methodology might be interviews or questionnaires. Your secondary research methodology might include studying website information and then comparing it with information obtained from textbooks.

In your notes you should consider and comment on certain methodological issues. You could use the following checklist to make sure that you are able to give a comprehensive description of your personal research methodology in the exam:

- Do my research findings include qualitative (opinion-based) or quantitative (statistic-based) information or both? How was the information used? If I used both types, was one more useful than the other?
- How did I go about collecting the information which was generated by primary sources? Did I expect questionnaires to be returned to me, for example, and was this method of collection effective?
- How was my secondary research organised? Did I research using one type of resource first, for example the internet, and then move on to another? Did I use library databases to find information specific to my research project title? Did I use search engines to ensure that my internet research was focused?
- How did I check the direction of my research? By reviewing it with my teacher, discussing it with members of my class, constantly referring back to the focus question, or all three?

Content
Guidance

This section outlines the main areas you should focus on in your preparation for the Unit 2734 Critical Research Study exam. It includes content information and key issues and debates for each of the topics available to choose from. The topics are broken down into subtopics for potential research focus. You could choose one of these in order to help you frame your question and complete your research. Alternatively, you could identify your research focus by merging two subtopics.

In order to ensure that the research you undertake is entirely independent, resource lists are not included. You should use this section as a guide to possible exam content and add your own thoughts and questions.

The topics are:
- women and film (p. 13)
- popular music and youth culture (p. 16)
- politics and the media (p. 19)
- children and television (p. 24)
- sport and the media (p. 30)
- concept to consumption (p. 32)
- community radio (p. 35)
- audience research (to be phased out after June 2004) (p. 37)
- crime and the media (p. 40)

Films that have an 18 certificate have been identified with an asterisk. The OCR Media Studies A2 specification allows the use of 18-certified films. However, if you choose an 18-certified film for your Critical Research Study, you should discuss your choice with your teacher before commencing your investigation.

Women and film

This topic is a popular option. It is a rich area, involving research into the relationships between female filmmakers and the film industry. The term 'filmmaker' is used to describe women working in any significant capacity in the film industry and can include directors, editors, cinematographers, producers, actors and set designers. You may decide to investigate issues connected with just one filmmaker or to consider a group of female filmmakers and the issues raised by their work or their position in the industry. One important point to remember, whatever your choice of question, is that the specification suggests that you consider a key 'relationship' — for example, between female filmmakers and film institutions, between films produced by female filmmakers and their audience, or between films not directed or produced by female filmmakers and the female spectator.

There is a wide range of areas which you could study under the general heading of 'women and film'. The areas of investigation outlined in the specification are covered below, along with questions which you might use as prompts in your research.

Equality of opportunity in the film industry

You could consider the difficulties and restrictions faced by female filmmakers. Very few female directors can command huge budgets for Hollywood products, for example, and one area of investigation might be the factors which have resulted in this situation. Kathryn Bigelow has directed big-budget features, e.g. *Point Break** (1991), *Strange Days** (1995), *K-19: The Widowmaker* (2002), but is she the only woman working in Hollywood who can secure the confidence of investors?

Alternatively, you might decide that there has been a positive development in how women are treated within the industry and may want to track an 'opening up' of the industry to female personnel. There may not be many female directors working in Hollywood today, but there are plenty of female producers. Why might gender equality have been achieved in production but not in directing?

You might contrast the experience of female filmmakers in the Hollywood system with that of women working in independent film production. Are there any significant differences? If your answer to this is 'yes', what factors have brought about this difference? Do lower budgets, higher levels of potential creativity, different target audiences and so on have an impact on the position of women making independent films?

If you opt to address a question exploring development or change over a period of time, try to limit the time-span. Some comparison between 'then' and 'now' is beneficial, but if you attempt to look at an area over an extended period of time your research project will lose focus.

Remember, too, not to fall back on vague generalisations. Your project should make specific reference to examples of female filmmakers and their experiences.

Gender representation in films

Don't rely on textual analysis alone if you opt for this subtopic. The specification requires you to focus on women *and* film, and if you lean too heavily towards textual analysis, without taking account of the factors which influenced the particular area of representation you are considering, your project will be too narrow in focus. A worthwhile approach is to use texts as the basis for wider comment on the changing (or unchanging) representation of women within particular historical contexts. For instance, you might consider the way in which the 'Bond girls' have changed during the course of the franchise and discuss the extent to which shifting social attitudes to women have (or have not) influenced the female characters within the James Bond films.

This subtopic focuses on film texts rather than female filmmakers, so you could study texts by both male and female directors. You might choose to focus on a particular genre of film, for example, and consider how the representation of female characters in that genre differs (or not) between male- and female-directed films. You might evaluate the extent to which audience expectations of particular genres influence the kinds of role played by women in films of that genre. You may find that the cost of a film and the producer's expectation of box-office receipts have an impact on the representation of female characters within a particular genre, regardless of whether the film has been directed by a man or a woman.

Make sure that you focus your research in a manageable way. A question which considered 'changes in the representation of female characters in film over the last 10 years' would prove too large and your project would lack investigative focus.

Feminist critical perspectives

This subtopic is often avoided because students assume that they will have to wade through vast tracts of difficult feminist criticism. This is not the case. The subtopic does not ask you to describe the emergence of feminist critical thought, but to comment on the relationship between criticism, the text and the audience. Obviously, your focus is still women and film, so you should comment on the usefulness of feminist criticism for evaluating the position of women in films and the film industry.

If you opt for this area of study, you need to investigate whether feminist criticism has had any influence on film production and audience response. Your analysis might consider the approaches and theories of different feminist critics or might look at how feminist criticism approaches certain groups of films. You could take a more contextually driven approach and discuss the dynamic between feminist criticism and films produced within a particular decade.

There are many feminist film critics whose work would provide an interesting basis for an evaluation of a feminist critical framework. You could consider the usefulness of Laura Mulvey's writing on narrative cinema, for example, as long as you bear in mind when her famous essays were written and how her theories may have developed or been superseded since the 1970s. You could use Tania Modleski's discussions of female characters within Hitchcock's films and evaluate whether her ideas have had an impact on the contemporary reception of Hitchcock's work. You might consider bell hooks's feminist discussions of black characters and film audiences, and look at the relationship between this area of criticism and the texts evaluated.

Audience reception of films by female filmmakers

A research project under this heading could cover films which are explicitly about the female experience or simply those which are the work of a female filmmaker. However, your project will be far more straightforward if you choose to evaluate films which are recognised by audiences as having a female focus, rather than films which might have been created by a female filmmaker but are not obviously about women. The key term is 'audience reception', and you will need to investigate audience expectations as well as audience response. Both academic and popular criticism can be referenced, and you should cite specific examples of responses from critics, amateur commentators or your peer group.

The commercial or critical success, or lack of it, of films by female filmmakers, and what this illustrates about audiences, is a potentially fruitful area for investigation. If you choose to research this area, the first stage of your study will be to choose an individual female filmmaker or a group of female filmmakers. You do not have to limit yourself to directors, but could include female producers, actors or editors as well. Once you have chosen your female filmmaker(s) and films, make detailed notes on your responses to the following questions:

- Are these films targeted specifically at female audiences?
- How do the publicity and advertising for these films help to define the target audience?
- Are these films from a particular genre, and if so, how are women usually represented within this genre?
- Were the films financially successful?

The next stage of your research should be to collect critical responses to the films you have chosen. Try to gather a range of responses (academic and popular) from a variety of sources (e.g. newspapers, magazines, fan-sites, official internet sites, television, DVD commentaries), so that when you come to discuss your methodology in the exam you can compare and contrast the usefulness of your different sources. Once you have gathered these critical comments, begin to deconstruct them. Consider whether there are any similarities in the comments made by academic and popular critics. Are the same features of the films discussed or do the reviews have different areas of focus? What do you consider to be the audience's expectations of films by female filmmakers? Do these have an impact on the comments made about the films?

Tips

There are many different areas to consider if you choose to research women and film, and the topic offers the potential for a thorough and interesting piece of individual research. However, there are some pitfalls to be avoided, namely:

- studying a single film. Your research will be too narrow and is likely to become a piece of textual analysis. Focusing on just one film will not allow you to show the examiner that you have taken institutional and contextual factors into account.
- creating a question which is too wide-ranging and does not have a specific focus. Define the limits of your question carefully. If you opt for a question which encompasses too many filmmakers, too many genres or too much time, your project will become difficult to manage.

Key words and phrases

filmmaker; director; producer; gender; Hollywood film; independent film; represent-ation; historical context; social attitudes; feminist criticism; audience reception; audience expectation; popular criticism

Popular music and youth culture

As with women and film, you must make sure that your question addresses the relationship between popular music and youth culture and does not become a study of just one of these areas. Ensure, too, that your study is not limited to comments connected with your personal taste. You may be a great fan of a particular type of music, but without adequate investigation of how this type of music 'interacts' with youth culture, your project will be little more than a fan review.

As with all eight of the Critical Research topics, the specification offers suggestions for areas which would provide an effective study. These are outlined below, with ideas on how to approach them.

The nature of youth culture and subcultures and their relation to mainstream popular culture

If you choose to investigate this area, you should begin by offering some definitions of the terms 'youth culture' and 'subculture'. You should not feel that any definitions you come up with at the outset of your project are set in stone, however, and if during the course of your research your initial definitions develop, this will provide evidence to the examiner that your conclusions have taken all your primary and secondary research into account. Your own informed and independent definitions of terms will indicate a level of personal ownership of your project which will impress an examiner.

Once your terms have been defined and you have chosen which youth culture and subcultures you are going to study, you need to investigate their relationship with the mainstream. Some acknowledgement of the complexity of this relationship is essential. Remember that sometimes youth culture or subcultures resist the dominance of mainstream cultures, sometimes they conform and in other cases resistance may predate conformity in the development of a particular subculture.

The easiest way to begin a study of this area is to choose a genre of music. Once you have done this, you will be able to investigate the audience for this type of music, its expectations, how that audience expresses its attachment to the subculture and to what extent the relationship between this subculture and mainstream culture is resistant. Consider whether the type of music you have chosen influences the attitudes, dress and actions of those who listen to it. You could also debate whether the attraction of this particular music is the music itself or the anti-establishment stance it takes. Did punk music become popular because of the music and the bands or because of the anarchic, anti-mainstream position it adopted? You might investigate what happens to the audience of a style of music when it crosses over into the mainstream. Does the profile of the audience change? How important to the marketing of a band or type of music is its oppositional stance to mainstream culture?

The relationship between the music industry and other industries

The other industries could be fashion, film, television, video, live performance, the internet and newspaper and magazine publishing.

This subtopic is extremely wide ranging and in order to avoid attempting a research question which will prove too vast, you should begin by defining your parameters clearly. In addition to identifying which of the above industries you will discuss, you will also need to specify the genre of music you will be studying, in order to ensure that your project retains focus.

As technology has advanced, so have the potential contexts in which a band or artist can be presented or promoted. The success of a band or artist is based on sales, and exposure is a key element in securing maximum sales. You should outline how the press, the internet, television, radio, VHS or DVDs work to expose the music you have chosen to its potential market. Once you have done this, consider whether the particular relationship you have chosen to study is, for example, mutually beneficial, counter to the subcultural origins of the style of music or financially rather than artistically motivated.

There are important questions which you will need to ask in order to investigate the 'relationship' you have chosen fully. If you have chosen a type of music which originally existed as a subculture, relying on basic types of advertising to promote itself, is it possible to retain subcultural credibility when the band, artist or music genre is discussed in national newspapers, appears on *Top of the Pops* or has an associated glossy magazine? Conversely, are there relationships with other industries which can preserve the integrity of the music and its subculture? If a style of music is played on the Radio 1 breakfast show, for example, does this have the same impact on the associated image and status of the music as airplay on Tim Westwood's show?

Issues of ideology and the representation of youth culture and young people

If you choose this subtopic, you should realise that although the heading does not include the words 'popular music', this is still an important part of your focus. Students often reject this type of question because of the word 'ideology'. Don't be afraid of this term. If you have had any discussions in class or with friends about why a band or group was presented in a particular way on television, in the press or in a magazine, and if you have considered how the attitudes of society influenced that presentation, then you already know what ideology is.

Again, a focused title is vital. You could choose any medium to investigate — newspapers, radio, television, the internet or magazines — and then select a particular style of music. You might choose a group of magazines which are associated with a musical genre — hip hop or thrash metal, for example — and then consider how the music, the artists, the fans and the associated lifestyle are represented in these magazines. You could investigate the extent to which these magazines' representations reflect or influence the youth market they target. Which came first, the fashion and lifestyle or the magazine representation of it? You might look at how the press chooses to represent your chosen music genre and investigate whether dominant social attitudes have had any influence on that representation. Are stereotypes used when certain papers discuss rap music, for example, and are they used because of moral panics attached to the lyrics or lifestyles associated with the music? You might decide to look at niche market products and compare these with more mainstream products. Do the fashions, attitudes and lifestyles attached to certain genres of music become diluted when they appear in mass-market publications?

Whatever section of the media you choose to investigate, you need to comment in detail on what you consider to be the 'voice' behind the representation being offered. What do you think has influenced the newspaper, magazine, radio or television programme? You may have chosen a newspaper which considers itself to be the 'moral guardian' of its readers, for example, and this would certainly have an impact on how youth culture and music are represented. On the other hand, you may have chosen a magazine which presents itself as being part of the youth subculture it is reporting on, in which case its motivation might be to reflect and promote, rather than to stereotype and warn.

Tips

There are several possible avenues for a detailed and well-researched project on popular music and youth culture. There are potential pitfalls, however. You should be careful to avoid:

- producing research which is fan-based or driven by personal response. You will need to retain some critical distance in order to investigate your topic fully.
- concentrating on a particular artist or band. Projects of this kind do not allow you to discuss your subtopic in enough depth.
- omitting a discussion of the relationship between popular music and youth culture and concentrating too much on textual concerns, such as lyrics and musicology. Consideration of a 'relationship' or a 'dynamic' is an essential part of a successful Critical Research Study.
- taking the term 'youth culture' as a given and not attempting a definition of its meaning. Examiners look for evidence that you understand the terms of your research.

Key words and phrases

popular music; youth culture; subculture; mainstream; genre; anti-establishment; oppositional stance; exposure; ideology; mass market; niche market; stereotype

Politics and the media

This topic is often unattractive to students, many of whom assume that they do not have the necessary knowledge and that any research connected to politics will be dry and boring. Try to set aside any negative preconceptions you might have. There are many subtopics within politics and the media which can produce an effective and interesting research project. You are not required to analyse policy or to discuss a political party, but to investigate the relationship between contemporary politics and the media texts which represent it. You could include *Private Eye, Brasseye* or *2DTV* in your research, or consider the impact and influence of political cartoons in newspapers. Although your focus must be contemporary British politics, there are few limitations on what you can study. You could even compare the relationship between the government and the media in the UK and other countries. Consider the subtopics below, as suggested in the specification.

Party political broadcasts, campaigns, photo-opportunities and lobbying

There is a wealth of possible research material for this subtopic, which could be derived from any medium. You should make sure that you extend any analysis of texts into a discussion of their intention and reception. Some evaluation of how (and to what extent) political representations are controlled by parties and the media is also necessary. You could focus on particular parties and trace their changing representations. You might also investigate how new technologies, such as the internet, and an increase in formats and contexts of reception, influence the impact of political messages.

There have been two general elections of which you may have some personal recollection (1997 and 2001) and these could provide a basis for your research. The campaigns associated with these general elections utilised every medium available in order to 'sell' the competing political parties to potential voters. In any town or city during these election periods you would have seen hoardings displaying posters urging you to vote in a particular way. These posters can be analysed in the same way you might analyse a film poster. They use colour, composition, text, representation and iconography either to promote one party or to discredit another. You could choose one party's poster campaign and consider the messages being relayed through its visuals, the intended meanings behind its visuals and the reception of these posters by target voters.

You could extend your investigation of a particular party's campaign by including party political broadcasts in your evaluation of how visual media are used by campaigning parties. Look at the studio setup, the colours chosen, the stance and position of the politician and the iconography which surrounds him or her in order to evaluate the party's strategies for engaging the viewer.

An investigation of how one political party's election campaign interacts with another's would also be a rewarding topic of study. Does there seem to be a 'dialogue' between the electioneering products used by the parties? Do particularly vehement attacks provoke a response from the opposing party? How does this kind of media battle affect the audience?

Public-service broadcasting and politics

An understanding of what public-service broadcasting (PSB) means is crucial for this subtopic. The ethos of PSB is to be devoid of commercial interest and thus commercial influence — it is supposed to reflect political events accurately, without putting forward a biased viewpoint. A research project could evaluate the extent to which this independent ethos exists in reality. Comment on how PSB has changed since its beginnings to become what it is today, and make sure that you engage with some of the debates within this area. The BBC, for example, as a public-service broadcaster, has a responsibility to remain free from political influence. However, there are regulations, put in place by governing political parties, which have an impact on the BBC. Does this mean that it can never be wholly independent?

You could begin a project by choosing a selection of programmes on BBC radio, BBC television or both, for example *Today* on Radio 4 and *Newsnight* on BBC2, which report on or discuss political events. You would then need to evaluate how the various political parties and personalities in Britain today are represented by the programmes. You could consider whether one party seems to be afforded more airtime than another, whether particular programme hosts seem to be more lenient or harsh with representatives of different political parties, or whether the news reports concerning particular political events seem to include a judgement or biased comment. Don't restrict yourself to studying the spoken text in television programmes. Analysing the camerawork, editing and *mise-en-scène* can be equally valuable in determining how a party or politician is treated.

Government press secretaries, public relations managers, spin doctors and the media

This subtopic focuses primarily on how political identities are formed and their level of 'constructedness'. The public image of a political party and its individual politicians is crucial, as an adverse image can undermine public confidence and may ultimately mean that a party is not elected to government. You could choose to focus on a particular party and investigate press release content and representations in the press in order to discuss the kind of media image being created. Alternatively, you might choose a particular event in contemporary British politics and assess the relationship between party statements and press representation.

Fundamentally, the role of press secretaries, spin doctors and public relations managers is to promote a political party or an individual politician and to foster and maintain positive public opinion. The extent to which the 'real' personality of the party or politician is conveyed by press releases and spin-doctor-influenced media coverage is debatable, and this question would form an interesting basis for a research project.

You could look at media coverage of a particular political event or a situation associated with an individual politician and consider whether the 'true' nature of the incident was addressed in the coverage. To what extent are controversial or potentially embarrassing events 'reworked' by a party's (or government's) 'spin machine'? A relevant recent case to consider might be New Labour's and Tony Blair's presentation of the evidence concerning Iraq's weapons of mass destruction, links with terrorism and contravention of United Nations resolutions as grounds for British participation in military action against Iraq in early 2003. Were the media employed to present the public with the facts, or manipulated to provide a misleading justification for the war?

Media commentators

How (and via which media) a particular party or political event is presented at any given point in history can provide the stimulus for very interesting projects. Media commentators may be individuals (such as particular journalists) or groups (for example, the team of people working on a radio or television programme), and the term encompasses satirists as well as traditional political analysts. Many students find satirists interesting and entertaining to research and write about.

A study in this field would need to identify key commentators or contexts for commentary and consider the impact that these might have on the political party or individual being talked about, as well as on the consumer. You could consider the extent to which the increase in different commentary contexts and the greater exposure received by politics nowadays has a positive or negative impact on the way in which political parties are viewed by the British public. Alternatively, an investigation into whether political commentary has any influence on the political parties on which it comments could form the foundation of an effective study.

To make sure that your research project retains focus, you should limit the number of media commentators you investigate. You could do this by restricting your research medium, focusing on press, radio, television or internet commentary. You might study one political party and consider cross-media commentaries. If you choose to look at the press, for example, an evaluation of the differences between broadsheet and tabloid commentary would be productive. You might look at the differences between political cartoons in a number of newspapers. What do you think is the intention behind the cartoons and how are they received by the reader? Do you think that these cartoons have any impact on the political parties they depict? You might consider the relationship between a publication such as *Private Eye* and the politicians it satirises. Does inclusion in an edition of the magazine provoke public ridicule or is it useful in bringing a politician to the public's attention?

Your study might identify some political discussion radio or television programmes and analyse them for format, delivery, target listener/viewer and political comment. A study of television would not need to be restricted to terrestrial channels; it would be interesting to investigate the different kinds of programme available via both satellite and digital channels. As with the press, you might decide to look at how television satire and comedy are used to comment on political events and personalities. Television impressionists, for example, are sometimes credited with keeping particular politicians in the public consciousness. If Rory Bremner stopped impersonating a particular politician, would it signal the demise of that politician's political relevance?

Impartiality versus editorial/owners' values

If you opted for this subtopic you would need to combine your skills of textual analysis with the knowledge of media institutions you have gained from your course so far. Political commentaries within news reports or news discussion programmes, for example, would need to be evaluated to determine the extent to which content is impartial and independent or influenced by those who commission the programme or own the means of production.

In order to get to grips with the idea of impartiality (freedom from bias), it might be productive to compare the reporting of news events and issues in a public-service programme with one which has been produced by a commercial company. Although government regulation has some influence over the content of public-service products, there is no individual 'owner' as there is in major media conglomerates. Consider how reports of political events and issues are presented on *Sky News*, for example, and then compare this presentation with a news programme from the BBC. Is it possible to detect the political bias or affiliations of Rupert Murdoch in the Sky reports, and does this give rise to a different picture of events from that offered by the BBC? You might analyse the language used in the two programmes, the footage of the events and the importance various stories are given in the running order. Does an owner influence the type of political coverage we are offered or the format in which it is delivered?

This subtopic does not restrict you to discussing the influence of media owners; the editor of a particular programme or newspaper might exert some influence over content too. Study the editorial section of a newspaper and try to identify the political stance, attitudes and values of the editor. Are his or her attitudes and values consistent with others expressed in the paper? Is there any evidence of editorial control? You could look at key individual editors and discuss their public profiles, their expressed political allegiances and their attitudes to current social issues. You could then evaluate the influence they may have on the content of political articles.

The relationship between media owners and government legislation

The relationship between media owners and government legislation is a complex one. To make your project as straightforward as possible, you should limit your discussion to either particular types of legislation or regulatory bodies that use government legislation. You could look at the 1990 Broadcasting Act and identify not only what it specified and how this was different from what had gone before, but also the changes in programming it caused and any resistance to it. You might investigate legislation connected to the use of new media technologies and consider the impact that this has had on how media owners can present content.

If you wanted to concentrate on regulatory bodies and the legislation which is associated with them, you might investigate the role of the Advertising Standards Authority (ASA) or the British Board of Film Classification (BBFC), and consider not only what kind of influence they have over media products, but also what kind of legislation they can invoke if a media company or organisation breaks any of their set criteria for content. Are there obscenity, child or animal protection laws, for example, which the BBFC can use to justify cutting or even banning a particular film? To what extent have changes in these types of law extended the potential influence of the BBFC?

Tips

You might now have an appetite for a project on some aspect of politics and the media. As with all of the topics for the Critical Research Study, however, there are key mistakes which you must avoid. Do not:

- rely too heavily on the representation of politicians in the tabloid press. You may already have notes on this area which you made in preparation for the Unit 2731 Textual Analysis exam, but resist the temptation simply to reuse them in Unit 2734: a focus solely on tabloids would render your project far too narrow.
- create a question which only includes discussion of the media's representation of previous political events, and does not include comparison with contemporary events and representations
- focus only on textual analysis. You need to engage with the wider implications of the relationship between politics and the media.

- create a project which describes political developments or changes and omits comment on the media's relationship with political events, individuals or systems

Key words and phrases

political cartoon; party political broadcast; election campaign; target voter; public-service broadcasting; commercial influence; independent broadcasting; press secretary; public relations manager; 'spin doctor'; 'constructedness'; public image; press release; media commentator; satirist; impartiality; editorial control; government legislation; 1990 Broadcasting Act; Advertising Standards Authority; British Board of Film Classification

Children and television

This topic attracts a significant amount of student interest. It is a huge area in terms of critical coverage and is multidisciplinary in the sense that you will be able to find academic comment from a sociological and psychological as well as from a media perspective. It's not a question of gathering up and regurgitating all of this critical writing. You need to show an ability to distinguish between what is relevant to your focus question and what is not. Try to make sure that you always retain a good balance between critical opinion and your own observations from primary research. The specification requires you to focus on the relationship between children as the subjects of media representation and children as television consumers, and you should remember that this dynamic is central to your study. Below are some examples of subtopics you might consider.

Children's television genres

Studies in this area should not assume that children's television genres are the same as adult ones. One research possibility could be to analyse definitions of adults' and children's genres, commenting on the similarities and differences. You may find that adults' and children's genres are completely different and follow dissimilar conventions, or that the generic headings are the same but the conventions vary.

You could also investigate the function of genre within children's television, and consider whether genre works to create familiarity through recognisable elements in the same way that it does for adult viewers. Do children have expectations of certain genres? Do they feel unhappy with their viewing experience if these expectations are not met?

Any study under this subtopic heading should evaluate types of genre and convention and discuss the impact on the child viewer of specific generic elements. The best way to obtain this information is to create focus groups of children who are the target audience for certain programmes. They may not have the vocabulary to define a convention, but they will certainly have opinions on what elements they expect to see in certain types of programme and how these elements affect them.

Advertising that targets or uses children

There are two different areas within this subtopic and you must distinguish clearly in your mind the difference between advertising which uses children to sell products to adults, and adverts specifically targeting children. To make sure that your project does not become unwieldy, you should focus on just one of these types of advertising.

Projects that focus on adverts which are specifically aimed at children should relate advertising strategies and product representation to audience reception and ideological concerns. If you concentrate on this area, you should use your existing analytical skills to consider how camerawork, iconography, editing, *mise-en-scène* and sound are used to engage the child viewer. Are common stylistic features evident within adverts for a particular target audience, across a range of products? Are there conventions within advertising for different age groups? If the adverts you have chosen for children's products use children, how are the children represented and what impact do you think this representation might have on the child viewer? Is a dominant social attitude towards children evident in the representations you see? Are the family setups in your adverts representative of a cross-section of families in Britain, or does the advert trade on the stereotype of the mother, father and two perfect children? Ask the children in your focus groups how 'normal' the family representations in the adverts seem to them. Don't forget that although the children may be the target audience for these adverts, it is their parents who will have to pay for the product. What strategies do you think the adverts use to engage parents?

Projects which look at the role of children's representation within adult advertising could follow a similar line, evaluating how representation informs our understanding of ideology. Try to choose a range of products which use children to sell to adults, and then analyse carefully the representation of childhood and children offered and how it affects the adult consumer. Does the advert invite adults to remember their own childhoods, ask them to evaluate their competence as parents, or use the image of a child to evoke an emotional response? Your primary research should include discussions with the target audiences of the products you have chosen. You may be able to contact the producer of the advert and ask questions about the rationale for using a child.

When your own textual analysis and primary research have been completed, begin to analyse contexts. Do the representations of children and childhood which are evident in your adverts indicate anything about dominant social attitudes towards children? Do your adverts use current social fears for, or perceptions about, children? Do you consider this manipulative or exploitative?

Representations of childhood and gender

As in any discussion of representation, you should combine textual analysis with a consideration of the producer's motivation for including certain representations in the texts you have chosen. Pay attention, too, to any dominant social ideologies which seem to lie behind the representations. In order to evaluate the ideological context of your chosen texts, consider whether the representations involve stereotyped or revised images of childhood and gender, and to what extent the images offered are consistent with majority social attitudes.

When choosing the focus for your study, avoid individual television texts. Instead, group together texts which you feel have a common thread; they might all use representations of children to target a particular age group of children or they might be for an adult market, and offer a particular representation of children. You could, for example, study a group of television programmes which use representations of children and are targeted at children, such as *The Tweenies* or *Rugrats*. Investigations of this type would need to evaluate the nature and purpose of representations and to discuss, for example, whether these perpetuate stereotyping or (at the other extreme) construct subversive representational models.

The extent to which children are passive or active consumers of the representations on offer is another interesting area of study. When conducting your primary investigations for this type of question, you should discuss your chosen programmes with members of the target audience and consider whether the values implicit or explicit in the representations offered have any influence on the opinions or actions of the children who watch the programmes. Do the parents of the children consider these representations stereotypical? Have the parents noticed any continuation of the representations of childhood and gender into their children's play or conversation?

If you select texts aimed at adults which use representations of childhood and gender, your investigations should follow a similar line. What are the messages concerning childhood and gender? Are these messages merely accepted by adult viewers or mediated by their own opinions and experiences? You could consider a text which seems to offer an idealistic representation of an untroubled childhood and discuss the impact the text and its producers seem to intend. You might look at texts which represent childhood as a period of uncertainty and vulnerability and discuss whether recent social fears concerning paedophilia have affected the way in which society now views childhood. Consider whether the gender of the child plays any part in the representation offered. Have the characteristics of boys and girls highlighted by media texts changed in any way in the last few years? If so, what do you consider to be the reasons for this?

There are three key stages to remember with any study of representation. First, what does the text seem to be suggesting through the representation offered? Second, what are the intentions behind the producer's choice of this particular representation? Third, how does the representation relate to social attitudes, fears and expectations?

Academic perspectives

Many students avoid this subtopic, and if projects do not have clear boundaries they can prove to be difficult. If you select a specific debate relating to children and television, however, and fix the boundaries of your project clearly, this can be a fascinating subtopic to study.

Whichever area of critical debate you select, you will need to make sure that you evaluate the relevance and usefulness of the studies you find (for example, psychological or sociological perspectives), rather than merely reiterating their content. The children and television violence debate is always popular, but it must be investigated fully. Too many students seem to start from the assumption that television images have a detrimental effect on children and do not cover the other side of the debate adequately. Don't forget that your task is not merely to relate the perspectives you have found to the examiner, but to evaluate and assess them, too. How have academic perspectives changed over time and why has this happened? Which do you think are the most effective and useful theories with regard to your chosen heading?

Television as education

One way of approaching this subtopic would be to distinguish between programmes which have an explicit educational agenda and those in which the educational content is more implicit. Debates concerning expectations, intention and reception become much clearer if this distinction has been made. Another approach could be from an institutional perspective — for example, evaluating the effectiveness of a PSB channel which includes an educational motive in its mission statement. You could investigate the medium of television as an effective teaching method, too, and compare it with on-line learning, for example, or CD-ROM educational packages.

As with all of the research areas covered in this guide, a clear focus makes for a manageable and effective study. If you concentrate on television programmes which have a clear intention to educate, begin by choosing a feasible number of texts. The BBC *Bitesize* series, for example, could prove an interesting area of investigation. Look at the strategies the programmes use to engage viewers and stimulate their interest in the topic being discussed. How are camerawork, presenters, *mise-en-scène*, editing and sound used to retain viewers' attention and make the content delivery effective? If your chosen programmes are less explicitly educational, you still need to investigate how the educational elements are presented. *Newsround* and *Blue Peter*, for example, have educational content but do not have the same education 'label' as the *Bitesize* series. What kinds of educational information do they contain and how effective do you consider their delivery of this information to be? The role of television in educating children about social groups, social dynamics and emotional issues would provide a useful research topic focus.

You do not need to confine yourself to evaluations of education about specific subjects. Do you consider soap operas or drama programmes as having educational value? Do these types of programme help children to understand the world around them or do they merely confuse?

Research on the effects of television on children

The 'effects debate' (i.e. discussion and disagreement concerning the impact of television on children) is far reaching and long running. A study under this subtopic should consider the various arguments in the debate and measure these alongside the conclusions you draw from your own interviews, questionnaires and research. Academic studies should be challenged and good projects comment on the method-ologies of the research which they encounter, as well as the findings.

The effects debate centres on two different viewpoints. The first is that children are passive consumers who are unable either to decode or to mediate what they view on television. In this model children become desensitised when shown violent images, for example, and are then capable of copycat behaviour. The media are held respon-sible for the desensitisation and problematic behaviour which might ensue from a child's viewing. The second viewpoint considers children to be active participants in the viewing experience. They have the skills to decode what they are watching, can tell the difference between fantasy and reality and can therefore deal with 'problem-atic' material in a way which does not encourage subsequent violent or troubled behaviour. According to this argument, the media are not to blame for children's behaviour patterns. If a child has a predisposition towards problematic behaviour, this may be made worse by certain types of viewing, but television does not 'cause' the child to act in antisocial ways.

It will be your task, if you choose this subtopic, to describe both sides of the debate, discuss the individual researchers who figure prominently, compare the two argu-ments with your own primary research findings and then put forward your evalua-tion and conclusions.

Children as participants in television programmes

Like children and advertising, this subtopic could be approached in two ways — either as a study of children's programmes which use children as participants or as an inves-tigation of how adult programmes use child participants. If investigating the former, you could study the relationship between child viewer and child participant, focusing on the role of identification as a means of engaging the child audience. If discussing the latter, projects could consider why children are used, what it is about them which engages the adult audience and whether this use is potentially exploitative.

You could compare and contrast the use of child participants in a selection of adult programmes and a selection of children's programmes. What are the similarities and differences in how children are represented in the two types of programme? How do the strategies used to engage the audience differ? If you decide that the children's programme encourages child viewers to identify with the characteristics, exploits or interests of the children in the show, does the adult show encourage adult viewers to remember their own childhoods, to reflect on the experiences of their own children or merely to laugh at the cute exploits of the children on screen?

Views of parents, teachers and children, effects debates, violence and theoretical models

This subtopic has a slightly different emphasis, in that it asks you to research the relationship between popular and academic criticism. You could consider parental attitudes to contentious issues connected with children and television, such as the effects debate, and comment on whether these have changed over the last few years. You might choose to investigate the extent to which academic criticism mirrors popular attitudes. The factors which influence adult opinion would be an effective area of study too.

If you select this area, you will need to interview parents, teachers and children. Children, of course, cannot be interviewed in the same way as adults and you will need to take care when framing questions which ask children to be reflective about their own viewing experience. Questions for parents should cover how personal experience has informed their views, how media coverage of the debates surrounding children and television has affected their opinions and whether their attitudes have changed since having children of their own. When interviewing teachers, ask how their observations of children in schools inform their opinions. You might want to choose teachers from different subject areas and evaluate whether the subjects they teach have any impact on the opinions which they express.

Once all of your primary and secondary research has been completed, draw your findings together in a consideration of the similarities and differences between the opinions expressed. What were the dominant opinions of the three groups of inter-viewees and what do you think were the factors which informed these opinions? Does the academic criticism which you studied reflect the opinions of the viewing public?

Tips

The sheer volume of views concerning children and television can be daunting. It is essential, therefore, that you focus both your question and your research. Do not type 'children and television' into a search engine, for example, as you will be faced with tens of thousands of results. Always ask specific questions, whether it be of a search engine, a library indexing system or an interviewee.

Types of project which you should avoid are those which:

- describe academic criticism without evaluating the different approaches
- concentrate entirely on violence and film, focusing on the moral panics attached to certain texts, e.g. *A Clockwork Orange* *(1973) and *Child's Play 3* *(1991)
- follow a predetermined agenda, e.g. that the media are culpable and television is detrimental to children, without considering both sides of the debate

Key words and phrases

children's television genres; conventions; expectations; target audience; advertising strategies; representation; dominant social attitude; consumer; social fears; manipula-tion; exploitation; stereotyping; subversion; passive and active consumption; mediation; educational television; implicit and explicit agendas; desensitisation; media responsibility

Sport and the media

This is a popular topic, but it is one that needs to be approached carefully. Students often choose this area out of personal interest, but it is important to make sure that objectivity is evident within your project; otherwise it will end up as merely a fan commentary. The specification emphasises the relationship between sporting agencies and the media. The study of your favourite football team, or a similar type of project, could never meet the relationship requirement.

As with any of the Critical Research topics, you will need to choose a specific area of research. The subtopics for sport and the media are listed below.

The attraction and retention of audiences to promote other products

Here you are asked to consider the means by which media companies attract and retain audiences via sport, and how other products, such as programmes offered by a TV broadcaster, are sold by taking advantage of this. You would need to describe and evaluate categories of attraction and retention methods, with reference to specific examples. You might look at the way in which new technologies, exclusivity and the range of sports offered on different channels are used as incentives. Are the features of digital programming, such as 'player cam', camera angle choice and commentary choice, significant to the decisions viewers make about their viewing of sports? Do pay-per-view events, such as boxing matches, encourage viewer loyalty? Do viewers today demand a range of sports viewing, including minority sports, and take this into account when choosing a viewing 'package'? You could use case study examples, such as Sky Sport, in order to substantiate your points, or perhaps conduct a comparison of terrestrial and satellite or digital packages. Television is, of course, not the sole medium for sports and you could consider radio programmes or sporting magazines too.

Organise your primary research in such a way as to investigate the expectations and consumption of the target audience for sports programming. Do consumers influence the range of sporting events available to choose from or do your interviewees consider that their choices are made for them? You might wish to comment on the profile of the audiences targeted by media companies and analyse whether or not they represent a cross-section of society. Your interviews and questionnaires should also reveal whether other products are effectively marketed through sport. What are these other products? Are they sport-related or other media texts? Are they promoted explicitly or implicitly by the company behind the sports presentation?

The representation of ideology

The kinds of issues you might consider in a project on this subtopic include global unity, nation and gender. In this context, 'ideology' concerns the messages and values that are implied through the presentation of sporting events. Do certain sporting events encourage viewers to see themselves as members of a global community? Do others encourage viewers to take pride in their nation?

This subtopic could either examine an individual sport or analyse a sporting event. You could investigate the Commonwealth or Olympic Games, for example, and consider their role in promoting national and global unity. An equally effective method of addressing this area would be to evaluate which sporting events are watched by men and which by women, considering popularity, availability and representation. Evaluation is key to a successful project, and you will need to decide if you think sporting events are an effective 'filter' for ideology and whether you think the ideologies apparent have a positive or negative impact on the audience. Do sporting competitions produce positive national pride or the kind of nationalism which involves hostility to other nations?

Minority sports

The term 'minority sport' encompasses a range of different sports for various target audiences and you should first settle on one minority sport as your focus. You should then examine the term 'minority' and consider whether this is connected to audience share or, perhaps more cynically, to profitability. An analysis of the place allocated to minority sporting events in schedules and the ways in which these events are advertised can provide the first point in a discussion about how media companies cater for minority markets. You could comment too on the role of new technologies, sponsorship and advertising within the 'treatment' of your chosen minority sport. Whatever minority sport you choose — from skateboarding to synchronised springboard diving — the process of investigation should be the same. Consider who makes up the potential audience, whether they are judged a profitable market option for media providers and how this is translated into scheduling, amount of coverage and the advertising which is allocated to the sport. Does your minority sport attract sponsorship? If it does, who are the sponsors and what does this indicate about the audience for the sport and potential profitability attached to it?

The use of new media technologies in sports coverage

The knowledge which you gained if you covered new media technologies in your AS course will be invaluable here. Studies on this subtopic should not just describe the new technologies available to sports audiences, but must assess their role in consumption modes, retention of audiences and advertising of products. A considerable amount of new media technology is used in the coverage of sporting events, including new reception hardware, such as set-top decoders and hard-drive recorders, interactive digital programme types and internet fan sites and advances in 'capture' technologies such as miniature cameras. A study of this area would need to question whether these new technologies have affected the way in which sport is consumed by its audience. Does the advent of interactive digital consumption mean that

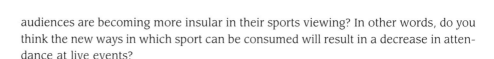

audiences are becoming more insular in their sports viewing? In other words, do you think the new ways in which sport can be consumed will result in a decrease in attendance at live events?

In answering questions of this kind you should consider both your own response and the opinions of other target consumers. How many members of your peer group use sport-connected new media technologies and how does this affect their response to live events? It would also be illuminating to consider how new technologies are used to promote media companies themselves. Look at the websites or advertising literature for these companies and analyse the comments and promises connected to new media technologies.

Tips

There are plenty of options in this topic for a focused and interesting project. Make sure, however, that you avoid the following:

- fan-based projects, which concentrate on a particular sporting hero or team
- purely text-based projects which offer deconstructions of (for example) sports programmes
- descriptions of sports media events such as the collapse of ITV Digital. This type of project tends to omit comment about audience
- projects which lack any discussion of ideology relevant to their topic area. The construction of 'nation' through sporting events is a particularly fertile area of debate which can be included easily.
- sociological commentaries, for instance on football hooliganism
- projects drawn from the tabloid and celebrity option in the AS Textual Analysis exam. An investigation into David Beckham's representation in the tabloids would not be appropriate for the Critical Research Study.

Key words and phrases

audience attraction; audience retention; new media technologies; digital programming; product promotion; global unity/community; national pride; nationalism; minority sport; scheduling; coverage; consumption modes; 'capture' technologies; interactive technologies

Concept to consumption

This option, though not particularly popular, provides a manageable and worthwhile avenue for student research projects. It requires a piece of comprehensive research into the processes involved in the production of a media text, from its conception to its consumption. You can choose a product from any medium — television, film, radio, the press, video or the internet — and the text can originate from Europe, the USA or other countries.

Your project should take the form of a case study, and you must make sure that you identify and evaluate all the stages of the product's 'growth', as well as showing understanding of the institutional contexts of its production and distribution. Your study should comment too on the 'success' of the media product. How is it received by its target consumer or audience? Does it fill a gap in the market or become swamped by other, similar products?

When choosing a text to study, try to be realistic. It will be much easier to obtain information if you either know somebody connected to the text or have easy access to personnel who may be able to provide you with relevant details. Investigating a local media text, such as a new magazine, newspaper, advertising campaign, music event, website or radio show, would be much more manageable than deciding to research the latest Hollywood blockbuster and then finding that you cannot access all of the information you need. You could investigate a local listings magazine, a fansite for a band, a regional television programme, a local radio show, a live music event, a short film, a video game or an advertising campaign.

In order to make sure that you have covered all stages, from concept right through to end product, your notes must include key types of information, which are covered below. Use the headings to check that you have all the necessary material.

Initial concept

The initial concept of the product is the first stage in any production process. It is usually modified during the course of production and you should make sure that you can trace its developments and discuss the influences (for example, costs or market forces) which led to any changes. Consider how the team or individual came up with the initial idea. Was it a response to a gap in the market or to audience research? You need to consider the aim of the product, too — for instance to improve the public profile of a company, to get a new company into the media marketplace or to retain the market position which a company already has.

Planning

The planning stage of any new project is crucial to its success and involves market tests as well as designing the product. Consider how your product was planned. Was planning a collaborative exercise or did the responsibility rest with just one individual? The time frame in which planning took place is relevant too. Was the amount of time allocated to planning prescribed by the production budget or were there no such constraints? Don't forget that you are supposed to be evaluating a product and you should comment on whether or not you think the planning involved was effective and efficient.

Personnel

Your notes on the personnel involved should include details of exactly who took part in the production process and what kind of influence each member of the team exerted over decisions. Who had most influence during the various stages of production and how did this affect the design and the target audience for the final product?

Technology

The knowledge of new media technologies which you gained through your preparation for the 2732 Audience and Institutions exam could be very useful at this stage in your research. Which technologies were used in the production of your chosen text? Were these new media technologies, and if so is the production of products such as yours only possible because of the recent advances in media-related technologies? You could discuss how the look and shape of the text are influenced by the technologies used to create it and consider to what extent audience expectations demand that certain technologies are used in the production of media texts in order to achieve a certain production standard.

Facilities

Examine the impact of the facilities available to the production team on the final product and its potential market success. Your product may have been produced by an institution with plenty of money and personnel, or it may be a low-budget enterprise, possibly even produced in somebody's home. If the product is a website and the creator has the appropriate software, limited facilities may not be an issue, but if the product is a film, lack of facilities may cause problems.

Time scale

The time scale of any media product's production is a useful indicator of the restrictions the production team was working within. If the time frame was limited, you will need to consider the factors which imposed the deadline. If your product had investors, for example, they might have wanted to get their money back from sales quite quickly. You should note too whether or not the production deadlines were met. If they were not, discuss how this affected the product's success.

Finance

The source of any financial investment for your product is an important factor, because it may have an influence on the look and content of that product. Try to find out what the financial sources were and consider what influence these sources may have had. You should try to discover whether the production team stayed within its budget, because this might have an impact on the final product.

Marketing

If a product is not marketed effectively it may not reach its potential target audience and may fail to make a return on any financial investment. You should make notes on what kind of marketing was used for your product. Did the campaign feature posters, articles or adverts in newspapers, internet pop-ups or flyers? You will need to use your knowledge of textual analysis and audiences to comment on how successful the advertising campaign was.

Distribution

Under this heading you will need to consider the breadth of distribution for your product and the rationale for that distribution. What were the contexts in which the final product was seen and were these contexts appropriate to the target audience? You should question too whether there were any controls on or limits to distribution and discuss how the type of product, its budget and the profile of the target consumer influenced distribution choices.

Consumption

The people who consume your product, and where, how, why and when they consume it, are important areas to consider. You could create a focus group of target consumers and discuss their reception of the finished product. Did it meet the expectations they have of this kind of product? Remember that you may fall into the category of target consumer and should note your own responses to the product you have chosen.

Tips

Once you have completed your notes under the headings outlined above and made sure that you have evaluated all stages of the production process, you should feel confident that you have everything you need to perform well in the exam. Remember, though, to avoid the following two pitfalls:

- choosing a product for which it is difficult to gain all the relevant information. Unless you have followed a well-known text and have collected all the necessary cuttings, reviews, data, etc., it might be difficult to offer a comprehensive research project.
- creating a project which relies too heavily on a single research source, such as the internet or a behind-the-scenes documentary

Key words and phrases

target consumer; target audience; gap in the market; initial concept; market forces; market position; market tests; collaborative planning; time frame/time scale; personnel; new media technologies; facilities; financial sources; marketing campaign; distribution; consumption

Community radio

This topic often produces extremely good responses. The focus of a project on community radio is an investigation into the relationship between radio stations and their communities, and a case study format is the best approach to take. There is a great deal of difference between the traditional notion of community radio (usually small-scale, possibly rural) and a radio community (a particular group of listeners with shared characteristics who have a loyalty to a particular show or station). Remember this distinction when you are considering which topic to choose for the Critical Research exam, as it may make this option seem more attractive. Some of the numerous avenues you could explore within this area are outlined below.

The nature and profile of radio communities

If you opt for this subtopic, you should concentrate on investigating the audiences for particular radio programmes and how they might constitute communities. Some radio stations connect with a community which already exists, while others define communities or foster a sense of community. If the example you have chosen falls into the latter category, begin by choosing a limited range of programmes and discussing which factors imply a consistent audience profile. What can you assume about the gender, age, lifestyle, interests and geographical location of the target listening audience? Consider the content of the programmes as well as their style of delivery.

When you have completed this textual analysis, you should move on to interviewing a selection of target listeners. What are their expectations about the content and delivery of radio programmes? Are these expectations met by the programmes offered on your chosen station? You will need to engage with the debate surrounding the function of a radio community, too. Why do listeners align themselves with a community? Does it foster a sense of safety or identity? Why is it in the interests of the programme or station to engender a sense of community — does it help to guarantee an audience?

The formation of radio communities

For this subtopic, you will be investigating the factors in play when a radio community is formed and the methods by which community identity is created or galvanised. Research projects should consider the role of age, geography, gender, nationality, fashion and sociocultural group in forming communities. The interaction between audience and programme is also important and you should consider language and cultural referencing (for example, to fashion or lifestyle) as a means by which the target audience is attracted. Does the programme you have chosen use language or cultural references which are only comprehensible to target listeners? If exclusivity is set up by the content of the programme, does it attract the target audience?

Try to work through the stages of community formation systematically, perhaps beginning with the strategies by which a new radio programme is advertised to the potential listener. How important is the presenter of the new programme in attracting listeners? How is the proposed content of the show used to attract listeners? Does the music used in a particular programme have specific connotations — for example, of youth and street credibility? Once you have evaluated the advertising stage, you should move on to the programmes themselves, examining cultural references and exclusivity.

Interviews with target consumers, and investigations into the introduction of the show and then the show itself, can all be used in your final conclusions. Do radio communities form independently, are they constructed by the programme or station, or is the process a mixture of both? If you consider your radio community as one which has been constructed, what is the impact of this on both the listener and the radio station?

Radio communities within public-service broadcasting

One possible starting place for a study on this subtopic is a consideration of the extent to which the creation of community is a guiding principle within PSB. You could use this debate as a way of introducing closer analysis of programmes and audiences. As with all of the topics in the Critical Research unit, an essential part of the initial stages is to define the parameters of your study; in the case of this subtopic, you should identify which PSB radio programme you are going to focus on. You might select, for example, the Tim Westwood rap show from Radio 1, or perhaps a show from BBC local radio. The second stage is to describe the profile of your chosen audience, giving details of age group, gender, ethnicity, lifestyle, expectations, listening habits and cultural background. Once you have defined the profile of your target audience, you should use your knowledge of the content, structure and delivery of your chosen show to consider whether the profile of the audience is catered for adequately by the PSB programmes which target them. The mechanisms, such as language, references and content choice, by which the programmes attempt to foster a sense of community, and the extent to which the interests of the target audience are mirrored in the programming, are essential questions for your project. Don't forget to keep referring back to the promises that PSB makes to its listeners. Is part of the PSB remit to cater for different community needs and do you think PSB achieves this, given the results of the research you have conducted?

Tips

If these descriptions of subtopic options have encouraged you to consider a study of community radio, bear in mind the methods for research suggested in this section and avoid projects which:

- describe your favourite radio programme and do not engage with any discussion of radio community
- read like a diary of work experience at a local radio station
- omit discussion of why radio programmes target specific communities

Key words and phrases

radio stations; radio programmes; radio communities; target listener; audience profile; expectations; content; delivery; cultural referencing; exclusivity; public-service broadcasting

Audience research

This topic asks you to investigate the ways in which audience research is carried out by media industries and/or academic researchers, and how it is used, whether by media institutions or in debates about the media. If you choose this topic, your task will be to investigate the research methods and then analyse their strengths and limitations.

Below are some ideas for potential areas of study, with guidance and subsidiary questions which you could consider.

Qualitative and quantitative methods

If you chose to look at qualitative or quantitative methods, it is absolutely essential that you understand the distinction between the two terms. Qualitative research is conducted by using focus groups, interviews and questionnaires which are analysed for opinion and experience, rather than for data. Conclusions drawn from qualitative research therefore evaluate responses and opinions, rather than statistical information. Quantitative methods are very different and record data, such as how many times a particular TV programme is watched, or involve carrying out questionnaires that provide a statistical outcome. The information gained from quantitative research is therefore statistic based.

Both methods are used by media industries to evaluate the impact and popularity of media texts and the range and profile of consumption. There are several approaches you could take to evaluate the effectiveness of these methods. You could focus on a particular media industry and investigate how it uses qualitative and quantitative findings, and conduct your own qualitative and quantitative studies into the same industry to assess the kinds of information gained and how useful it is. Alternatively, you could study the ways in which a particular media industry gathers data. Television viewing data are collected by the Broadcasters' Audience Research Board (BARB), an independent organisation that evaluates quantitative data and then feeds the results back into the industry. Television-viewing data are collected by placing data recording boxes in a selection of homes; the data recorded are analysed to discover which channels are viewed the most, which programmes are most popular with which members of a family, and what times of day viewing figures are at their largest. Another approach could be to analyse the effectiveness of quantitative data gathering, and to compare it to the effectiveness of qualitative information gathering processes such as focus groups, interviews and questionnaires.

The purpose of industry and academic research

This type of project should begin by identifying some examples of industry and academic research and then discuss their purpose. You might confine yourself to a particular media industry, for example television, radio or the press, and then identify both the research that particular industries carry out and the academic work which is associated with it. You will need to discriminate between qualitative and quantitative research findings, and then consider how each is used. The emphasis of this subtopic is on analysing how research results are used, not evaluating the effectiveness of qualitative and quantitative research-gathering procedures. Radio listening statistics are gathered by Radio Joint Audience Research (RAJAR), for example, and you could evaluate how the quantitative results gathered by this independent data-gathering organisation are used by radio stations. Consider the following questions:

- Is the purpose of research to analyse retrospectively the impact of media texts or to inform the creation of them?
- Does industry and academic research work in a regulatory way, checking and assessing the kinds of texts produced, or can it be used to justify decisions that have already been made?
- Is the purpose of research to provide information for the general public or solely for the media industry?

Moral panics

The first stage of any research project which evaluates moral panics is to ensure that you understand fully what the phrase means. A moral panic ensues after five different stages:

(1) Something or someone is defined as a threat to values or interests.
(2) The threat is depicted in an easily recognisable form by the media.
(3) There is a rapid build-up of public concern.
(4) There is a response from authorities or opinion makers.
(5) The panic recedes or results in social change.

Both words in the phrase 'moral panic' are highly emotive. For a threat to be moral, it must be seen as a threat to the fabric of society itself — something which is capable of destroying the social order. A panic is an extreme event, so a moral panic is a dramatic response by society to a threat that it perceives as potentially destructive.

To create an effective project on moral panics, you need to evaluate the stages of the process and what the social function of a moral panic is, and to identify and discuss examples of moral panics. Ask yourself evaluative questions:

- How useful are moral panics in dealing with social concerns?
- Do moral panics demonise the media and absolve others from social responsibility?
- Are the social and legal changes which happen as a result of moral panics effective and do they have appropriate targets?

The most effective way to carry out a research project into moral panics is to identify an example and then investigate the process of its creation. Moral panics concerning the impact of the lyrics of artists such as Eminem and Marilyn Manson make for an interesting case study. Consider how these artists have been blamed for certain events, and how the press reported on events for which these artists have been held partially or fully responsible. What was the outcome of the moral panic? Do you consider the panic to be at all legitimate?

You could consider whether or not you think moral panics are originated, sustained or accelerated by 'interested' groups. You will need to use specific examples in order to illustrate points, but your project should not be solely descriptive. The focus should be on the context of the panic, the motivation behind it and the outcome. A description of the events surrounding the James Bulger trial, for example, would not in itself be enough.

Effects research

This is an enormous field, and you will need to focus on a particular aspect of effects research. You may decide to investigate audience responses to media violence, how audiences consume different types of media text, or how the effects of media texts may change from childhood to adulthood. Once you have chosen your topic and collected relevant information, you should discuss the effectiveness of that research:

- Do you think the information you gathered expands your knowledge concerning the ways in which media texts affect their audiences?
- Do the effects research available and the conclusions drawn tell you anything about the perception of the media at a given point in time?
- Have effects debates concerning your chosen area changed over the years? If they have, why?

The key to a thorough project on this subtopic is to evaluate and challenge the effectiveness of the research you have identified and not just describe it. You could consider uses and gratifications theories, for example, but you would need to consider carefully how useful and relevant this type of research is. Your own primary research for this subtopic could include setting up a focus group (to discuss a particular type of media product, for example) and then using a uses and gratifications model to evaluate your own findings. You should then consider how useful a uses and gratifications approach has been and whether it imposed any limits on the way in which you evaluated your findings.

Tips

The key to creating a comprehensive project under this heading is to be extremely focused. You will need to generate a specific, as well as manageable, title for your project. Make sure that you avoid:

- confusing key terms. You should be absolutely clear on the difference between qualitative and quantitative methodologies, for example.
- lack of focus. Projects which lack focus become generalised reports or do not reference specific media industries.

Key words and phrases

media industries; academic researcher; quantitative methodology; qualitative methodology; focus groups; interviews; questionnaires; range of consumption; profile of consumption; BARB; RAJAR; moral panic; effects research; uses and gratifications models

Crime and the media

There is scope for a wide variety of research questions under this topic heading, but you should remember that you are being asked to investigate the dynamic between crime and the media. Your study should discuss how media texts represent either real or created crime stories and how these representations inform our understanding of social and institutional attitudes towards crime. The specification permits the study of representations of crime across a range of British media, but don't forget that focus is a key element to the success of your project. Below are some ideas for possible areas of study.

UK crime films

The most obvious point to make about any Critical Research topic connected with film is that your project should not be based on textual analysis alone. You need to discuss the context of any crime-related films you choose, as well as their textual content, and to consider the extent to which audience expectations and profitability influence the types of crime depicted. You might decide to focus on the new wave of British gangster films, from *Lock, Stock and Two Smoking Barrels** (1998) onwards, which would require a consideration of the tradition of British gangster films which these newer examples fit into, and a discussion on whether the representations of criminals in these newer films are consistent with what has gone before.

You could look at how the representations of criminals in your texts are received by different audiences. Don't forget to consider all of the factors which play a part in any representation: *mise-en-scène*, music, actors, camerawork, narrative type and editing. You will need to debate the reception of represented groups carefully. Is the 'cool' gangster image and the stylised violence evident in many modern gangster films received by all of the viewers in the same way? Do these kinds of representation affect how the films' audiences then view actual crime and criminals? You might even extend your analysis of UK crime films to consider whether the representations of crimes and criminals offered seem particularly 'British' in any way.

UK television crime series

You will need to limit yourself to a manageable group of texts when researching this subtopic, and one way of doing this would be to select crime series which have characteristics in common. You could choose programmes which focus on a group of officers or investigators, e.g. *The Bill* (ITV) and *Waking the Dead* (BBC1). You might focus on shows which pivot around an (often maverick) individual, such as *Silent Witness* (BBC1), *A Touch of Frost* (ITV) or *Inspector Morse* (Carlton). Alternatively, your choice of texts could be defined by their focus on police investigations, their use of prominent female characters or the particular location in which they are set.

Once you have chosen your texts and focus, you need to make a careful analysis of the representations offered. Do the crimes investigated in the programmes tap into current social fears? Do the groups represented — criminals, women, police officers, and so on — seem realistic, or is there dramatic licence in their depiction? Discuss whether the representations in your programmes make serious contributions to ongoing social debates or merely exploit current social concerns and fears in order to attract viewers.

True-crime magazines

There are many magazines which feature articles about true crimes and their investigations. If you choose to focus on a selection of these, remember that you will be studying not only the representations of crime offered, but the reasons why such magazines exist. A magazine series such as *Real Life Crimes...and How They Were Solved*, for example, could be investigated in a number of ways. First, you could study the readership of the magazines. Why do people buy them? It may be that they like putting themselves in the position of detective or they may enjoy the voyeurism of reading about crime. Do readers consume any other types of crime-related media products, such as television series? Your research should then extend to the content of the magazines. Consider the language which is used to discuss the crimes. Is it emotive and dramatic, or does it report the crime in a more detached way? How are the criminals portrayed? How are the victims of the crimes described? You should also look at the types of visual image contained in these magazines and consider whether they guide readers towards a particular response.

Next, extend your investigations beyond the text itself and discuss the function of these types of magazine. Do they aim to increase public awareness about particular crimes or is their function purely to make profit? The last stage of your study should evaluate the ideological issues surrounding these magazines. If they tap into a public fear of certain types of crime and criminals, you will need to consider whether this fear is justified and whether true-crime magazines serve an ideologically sound purpose.

Press representations of crime and criminality

Crime and criminality take up a good deal of press space and you will need to create a solid focus for your project in order to avoid simply producing a list of stories. You might decide to look at the different representations of crime in tabloid and broadsheet newspapers, comparing the information related, the tone of the articles and the response which the articles seem to be encouraging in readers. You also need to consider any bias which the chosen newspapers might exhibit. Their viewpoints on punishment, for example, give an indication of their overall attitude to crime and criminality. You might wish to choose one particular newspaper and evaluate its coverage of crime. Does it claim to be a 'social guardian'? Do crimes against property receive different treatment from crimes against individuals? You might consider culpability in your analysis too. Does the paper you have chosen consider social or psychological issues as part of its representation of a criminal? Does it blame violence in films and television programmes for violent crime? Your primary research should also include the opinions of readers. What attitudes do a particular newspaper's readers have towards crime?

Your final conclusions should bring together all of your research and consider whether press representations of crime perform a social function, whether they incite moral panic or whether they are constructed in order to gain and retain readers. You may find that your conclusions include all of these elements.

Crime in video games

You will have no problem finding secondary sources if you choose this subtopic, as it is a much-covered issue. To avoid being swamped with too much resource material, select a small group of games as your focus. Try to choose games which have similarities. You might look at games in which the player is positioned as a detective, such as *Max Payne*, or those which allow the player to commit the crimes, such as *Grand Theft Auto: Vice City*. With any video game-related question, consideration of how interactivity affects the player is essential, and you will need to incorporate this into your primary research. Try not to limit your investigations by reaching foregone conclusions concerning the effect of playing games on the player. If you align yourself too early in your study to either of the 'effects theory' models, you are likely to distort your observations and findings. Your own primary research, alongside any secondary writings, should inform your conclusions.

The focus of your study is how crime is represented and you should consider whether your research indicates a representation of crime as dangerous, fun or maybe a mystery to be unravelled.

Tips

The topic of crime and the media has plenty of scope and could easily form the basis of a challenging research study. However, project types to avoid are those which:
- attempt to cover too many texts. These are likely to become vague and to lack critical focus.
- rely too heavily on textual analysis and omit discussion of context
- begin with preconceptions concerning the impact of representations of crime on consumers

Key words and phrases

crime film; gangster film; representation; realistic depiction; dramatic licence; true-crime magazine; voyeurism; public awareness; social fears; ideology; tabloid; broadsheet; 'social guardian'; interactivity; effects debate

Questions
&
Answers

This section of the guide comprises sample question 1 and question 2 answers for the four most popular topics — women and film, popular music and youth culture, children and television, and sport and the media. For each topic, both the research-based question and the analytical question are answered. Two of the topics are answered at A-grade standard, and two at C-grade standard. It is important that you use these answers as a structure and style guide rather than as model answers for content. Consider the language used, the organisation, and the way the arguments are structured. These elements will be of most use to you when you are preparing for the exam.

Examiner's comments

Each of the candidate answers is accompanied by an examiner's comment, preceded by the icon **e**. These comments indicate what is creditable within the answers and why a grade A or C would be awarded. Pay particular attention to the strengths and weaknesses identified by the examiner, and treat the examiner's comments as useful advice in your preparation for the exam.

Women and film

(1) Describe and discuss the research methodologies you used to investigate your question.

■ ■ ■

Grade-A answer

Before conducting my research, I decided to narrow my topic down to romantic comedies, as I am aware of the wide range of genres within the film industry. I began researching my topic by watching a segment from the documentary *Reel Women*. This documentary illustrated to me that it is difficult for female filmmakers to succeed in male-dominated Hollywood. Although this documentary was not specific to my topic, it offered me a starting-point and gave me ideas of questions which I could use in my questionnaire.

I piloted my questionnaire on a few of my friends to test if it was appropriate and easy for them to understand. From this piloting, I had to make some changes to the wording because they did not understand media terms, such as ideology. After these changes, I used my questionnaire on a group of male and female subjects, aged between 18 and 55 years, mainly from social classes B, C1 and C2. I asked 25 people to fill in the questionnaire. I handed out the questionnaires and waited while the subjects filled them in. This was time-efficient, ensured that the questionnaires were filled in and enabled the participants to ask questions if they needed to. I used a combination of open and closed questions. The closed questions were appropriate for some things, e.g. 'Are you interested in romantic comedies?' The open questions provided much more detail and allowed the participants to elaborate on their responses. The results highlighted many differences. For example, 75% of the females were interested in romantic films and only 15% of the males were. The questionnaire was also useful in showing me the participants' values, and indicated that female directors are not well known as only 18% of participants could name a female film director. However, the sample size was small and may not be representative of the general population.

In order to obtain more detailed responses, I decided to organise a focus group. The group was made up of three males and three females, aged between 18 and 25. I used a dictaphone and video recorder to record what was said and the accompanying body language. The focus group was held at my house and provided me with much more detailed responses. One of the discussions was the importance of female appearance in film. The group concluded that appearance was a much bigger issue for women in film than for men, with the focus being on slimness and youth. The focus group allowed me to guide discussions and bring up issues relevant to my study. One of the issues raised was female film directors, and again the group found it difficult to name any. Only one member of the group came up with a name — Nora Ephron

— and it was significant that this member of the group was female. Although the focus group was useful and provided me with detailed responses, again it was small-scale.

I then e-mailed two people in the hope of a response. I first e-mailed Dr Martha Lauzen from San Diego University, but did not receive a reply. Second, I e-mailed an address I found on a website (**www.5050summit.com**) and this proved successful. The response informed me of the New York Women Film and Television (NYWFT), a non-profit organisation, run by women and set up so that women can buy tickets for films directed by women on the opening weekend. The e-mail also listed organisations that have been set up to support female film directors, but unfortunately most of the addresses were in New York, so I could not contact them.

I then conducted my secondary research. I started this by reading *Studying the Media* by Tim O'Sullivan. This textbook was of a suitable standard, easy to understand and designed for A-level students. It informed me of various audience-related theories, such as the 'uses and gratifications' model, which suggests that people use media texts for four reasons: surveillance, to gain information; for personal relationships (they can relate to the character); for personal identification (the media text can make a statement about them); and for diversion, offering them an escape. Although the media textbook was useful, it mainly discussed the role of women in magazines and advertising, not in film. I also looked at *Films for Women* by Charlotte Brunsdon. This book was at slightly too high a level for me, but was very interesting. It discussed the new women's film, which addresses itself to women. The only aspect of the book which I did not find useful was its concentration on women in film in the 1960s, which is not relevant to my topic area. In addition, many of the debates the book tackled were very complex.

I looked at other books too. *Feminism and Film* by E. Ann Kaplan illustrated the problems female film directors face in getting funding, as they are often associated with tackling difficult or controversial subject matter. Although I found this book quite useful, its focus on *film noir* was not very relevant to my topic. I also looked at *Feminist Hollywood: From 'Born in Hames' to 'Point Break'*. Although it only focused on three female film directors, it showed me the diversity of the films which these women have directed. The book was written by Christine Lane, who argues that Hollywood products are created in order to make a profit and have global appeal. Although this book was useful, it did not focus on romantic comedy. A book which I found to be more specific to my focus was *Popular Cinema* by Fiona Sage and Eyisha Mohammed, which discussed the conventions of romantic comedy. It demonstrated that romantic comedies stick firmly to the traditional happy ending, that marriage is seen as the best solution and that sex is now seen as separate from marriage and can be just for pleasure. This offered me a different perspective and again focused more on contemporary films.

The books I used were not always up to date and it was difficult to find information that was relevant to my topic. The internet was an important source of my research, as it was up to date and allowed me to refine my focus. One of the websites I used was **www.hollywoodnet.com**. This focused on the historical context of women in film, showing how the representation of women in film has changed dramatically over the years, from screwball comedy, to *film noir* and the modern era. Another very useful website was **www.5050summit.com**, which provided me with statistics about female producers, directors and executive producers. From this I found the 'celluloid ceiling' study, which analysed 2,462 employees from the top 250 films of the year 2000. The study found that 93 of the top 100 films had a male director. It also indicated that female directors are most likely to be seen within the romantic comedy genre, in comedy drama or animations.

Another useful resource was **www.wif.org**, which listed (chronologically) the achievements of female film directors. An extract from the *Encyclopaedia of Female Filmmakers* stated that women have lost their ground as filmmakers, having been more prominent in the past. The internet was also useful in finding information about feminist film theory. For example, I found 'Visual Pleasure and Narrative Cinema' (1975), an article by Laura Mulvey, in which she explained the voyeuristic way in which men look at women in film. The article suggests that women are passive objects and males are active and control the action.

I also used websites (**www.amazon.com** and **www.imdb.com**) to obtain synopses of the films I was using for my textual analysis. I carried out textual analysis of four films: *Bridget Jones's Diary* (2001) directed by Sharon Maguire, *You've Got Mail* (1998) directed by Nora Ephron, *Erin Brockovich* (2000) directed by Steven Soderburgh, and *Pretty Woman* (1990) directed by Gary Marshall. I chose these films as they are all mainstream Hollywood films that received widespread distribution. I wanted to compare the representation of women in each of these films and identify any differences in representation between the films directed by men and those directed by women. I watched all of the films three times, setting myself questions to answer in the second and third screenings.

e Evidence of a confident and thorough research process is demonstrated here. The candidate challenges sources and procedures as well as making good use of them. The materials have been selected appropriately.

(2) What were the conclusions you came to following your investigation of your topic?

■ ■ ■

The aim of my research was to investigate representations of women in films made by female and male directors. My questionnaires highlighted the values of the participants and the attitudes that they had towards women in film. I found a difference in attitudes between the males and females that I asked. Only 15% of the males had an interest in romantic comedies, whereas 75% of the females expressed an interest. This supported the view that romantic comedies are of interest to, and are targeted at, female viewers. I found that the males and females had different attitudes to the representation of women in film. This issue was of greater importance to the females.

I asked them to rate how happy they were with the representation of women on a scale of 1 to 10. The average score for males was 8, whereas the average score for females was 5.5.

The main focus of my research was the role of women within the filmmaking industry. Both the questionnaire and the focus group showed that filmmaking was predominantly male. The information that I gained from the internet (from the 'celluloid ceiling' study) also demonstrated that filmmaking today is still a male-dominated industry. The number of films made by women in 2000 constituted only 11% of the total. However, although this figure is low, it had risen from the 1999 figure of 5%.

I wanted to investigate whether there was any difference in the ways female and male filmmakers represented women. I analysed four mainstream romantic comedies. The first of these was *Bridget Jones's Diary*, directed by Sharon Maguire. The film challenges certain stereotypes in that Renée Zellweger, who plays Bridget Jones, had to put on weight for the film, so Bridget is not represented as supermodel-thin. The audience sees the film from her point of view and she appears in each scene. The film has hints of feminism in that Bridget is quite an independent woman, with a career, and she is seen out of a domestic role. However, the film reinforces traditional stereotypes of women, in that Bridget is seen searching for a man and is unhappy on her own. Bridget is eventually rewarded with a heterosexual relationship that makes her happy. This may be because female filmmakers cannot be too feminist in their representation of women, as they want to be accepted in the industry and need to attract funding and appeal to a mass audience.

When I compared *Bridget Jones* with *Pretty Woman*, directed by Gary Marshall, I found that the latter film reinforces female stereotypes and patriarchal values. Richard Gere's character is a successful Wall Street businessman, whereas Julia Roberts's character is a prostitute. The film reinforces the subordinate role of women, in that Julia Roberts's character is swept into a world of luxury and fantasy by the rich older man. Again, this film conforms to the conventions of the romantic comedy genre, as they end up 'happy ever after'. The female character is saved by the male character and rewarded with a heterosexual relationship. In comparing these two films, I felt that the representation of the female in *Bridget Jones* was much more positive than in *Pretty Woman*, the former film being directed by a woman. However, the fact that both are mainstream films influences their ideology.

I also compared *Erin Brockovich* by Steven Soderburgh and *You've Got Mail* by Nora Ephron and I was surprised to find that the representation of the female character was more positive in the former than the latter. In *Erin Brockovich* Julia Roberts plays an independent and strong-minded single mother. The fulfilment she gains from motherhood and her career challenges stereotypical views of women being unhappy without a man. However, at the same time there is an emphasis on her appearance, as she wears very skimpy clothes. In contrast, Nora Ephron's *You've Got Mail* sees the central female (played by Meg Ryan) portrayed less positively. Meg Ryan's character's business fails because of the economic power of the male protagonist (played by Tom Hanks). In this film, the male character is seen to be powerful and dominant and the story unfolds around him. When I asked people in a questionnaire whether they thought that a female was more likely to be represented positively in a film directed by a woman, 65% said 'yes'. However, from my own textual analysis it is clear that this is not always the case.

From my research, I have found that the position of women in the filmmaking industry has improved. However, access to the means of production is much harder for females to achieve. Women have to compromise and conform to the requirements of popular film. Women within the industry may have become more prominent, but there is very little recognition for their active roles. Laura Mulvey's gaze theory argues that women are presented as passive in film. They are purely objects of desire or pleasure for the male spectator. Levy's research in *Studying the Media* tends to support this. Emmanuel Levy researched Hollywood film stars and found that physical appearance was much more important for females. Age was part of this too; Levy found that the median age for females in Hollywood was 27 years whereas it was 36 years for males. This research makes apparent the sheer inequality that remains in Hollywood and Levy himself says that 'it shows no signs of changing'. However, at the same time independent women are represented in film, which is not a recent phenomenon. Katherine Hepburn played independent female roles in the 1930s and Linda Hamilton played an action heroine in the second *Terminator* (1991) film. In addition, since the 1980s there seems to have been more display and sexualisation of the male body.

From the focus group, I found that the film industry is still very much male-dominated. Feminists see this as reflecting a patriarchal society and contend that cinema has a negative impact on the female spectator.

e The candidate exhibits a sense of ownership over the research, as findings and research are clearly related to the wider topic. The evaluation is consistently strong.

e **These responses are challenging and well-referenced. The candidate provides a sophisticated commentary on the detailed research undertaken, and would be awarded a grade A.**

opic 2

Popular music and youth culture

(1) Describe and discuss the research methodologies you used to investigate your question.

■ ■ ■

Grade-C answer

I researched the relationship between hard house music and youth culture and how it evolved. First, I would like to define 'popular music' as music that a large number of people listen to, which is popular enough to sell in shops and to have a large audience. Second, I would define 'youth culture' as the younger generation. In my study I am researching the culture of this generation — their family, friends and life — and how it is affected by music.

There are two means of research — primary and secondary. Primary research is when you observe what you are researching. It is more reliable than secondary, but depends on the skill and technique of the observer. Diaries are a good source for this, as they give you exactly what the person thinks in private. Interviewing is also good, but it takes a skilled interviewer to retrieve the right information. This decreases reliability but increases validity. Questionnaires are also a worthwhile method of primary research. However, it takes skill to ask the right questions. The interviewer should not ask loaded questions or those which have a built-in answer.

Secondary research can involve going to a library. Books can be very helpful, but they usually record just one person's findings or beliefs, and are therefore less reliable. The internet is easy to access and use, but very unreliable and not always valid because anyone can make a website and put whatever information they want onto it. This information may not be true. Textual analysis also relies on the observers and their ability and is less reliable.

These are some of the research methods which can be used. I used observing, interviews and questionnaires, along with library, internet and textual analysis. I made up two questionnaires, one with five questions and one with eight. This was intentional, so as not to bore the interviewees. Both questionnaires asked about the interviewees' preferred music and where they listen to it, the second concentrating on hard house music. This method of research proved to be reliable and interesting.

I then set about researching how hard house has evolved over time and what youth culture has to do with it. I used books, the internet and television documentaries, and found a large amount of information. There are many books or websites which give an opinion of how hard house came about, but I concentrated on the most common story.

e This response starts well, with a definition of terms, and offers a competent evaluation of methodology. However, it should have referred to actual sources in specific detail to gain the marks available for thorough and appropriate detail.

(2) What were the conclusions you came to following your investigation of your topic?

■ ■ ■

Does popular music shape youth culture? Or does youth culture shape popular music? People change from year to year and so does music, but 'popular music' is only popular because people go out and buy it. So it is the youth culture which decides what is the popular music of the moment.

Hard house evolved this way, originating as disco in 1977 with John Travolta in *Saturday Night Fever*. This type of music became popular. Club promoter Rob Williams brought DJ Franky Knuckles from New York to DJ at his new club, The Warehouse. He played this new style of music, bringing black, white, straight and gay people together. People would go to stores asking to buy 'warehouse' music, which was shortened to 'house' music. Soon the limited supply of music meant that DJs had to be creative: 'they would find certain parts of a record that the crowd went mad for and repeat it' (*Pump Up the Volume* documentary for Channel 4). To be more creative, DJs started to add drum machines to the tracks.

In 1983, at Club Music Box in Chicago, Ron Hardy, known as 'heart attack Hardy', took clubbing to a new level. He was a very creative DJ and at the beginning of every set he would shout out 'Welcome to the Pleasure Dome'. Ron Hardy was a regular heroin user. While DJ-ing he would have been experiencing euphoria, drowsiness, respiratory problems and nausea. To him his music sounded slow, so he would speed it up. This new music was faster and harder.

Every Chicago youngster with a drum machine was then making music. Larry Sherman from Trax Records would buy up unsold records, break them apart and create new music. Club kids would abuse the drum machines made for karaoke. Earl 'Spanky' Smith and DJ Pierre made a tape from this. Ron Hardy played a tape of this and 'acid' music was born. In the 1990s this became hard house — a much deeper version with a distinctive sound. It is funky, energetic and bouncy. It has heavy and fast driving beats, melodic breakdowns, horns and synthesisers. Today's DJs, for example Fergie, Judge Jules and Rachel Auburn, are all making a living from DJ-ing hard house music. This shows how popular music has shaped youth culture, but I also believe that youth culture can shape popular music.

The type of people who listen to hard house are collegians (Frith's term) aged between 16 and 28, artistic and very creative. They do not listen to hard house for credibility and are not easily manipulated into buying merchandise. Music is very transient and hard house listeners appreciate it for what it is, rather than trying to see some meaning in it. However, people such as 'bubble-gum' listeners who listen to mainstream boy bands are easily manipulated into buying merchandise.

This shows how popular music can shape youth culture, because typical 'bubble-gum' listeners will all have similar clothes, shaping them into a category, whereas hard house listeners are creative and express themselves in an individual way.

🖉 This response is stronger than that for question 1. It attempts to describe the evolution of the chosen style of music and offers a fairly detailed description of the factors which influenced this development. The candidate draws some reasonable conclusions, but reference to criticism or theories would have gained extra marks.

 Overall, this response is sound, and shows evidence of the candidate's engagement with the topic. More marks could have been gained by producing a more sophisticated argument, and above all by referring to specific sources in depth. It would be awarded a grade C.

Children and television

(1) Describe and discuss the research methodologies you used to investigate your question.

■ ■ ■

Grade-A answer

For my Critical Research project there were three key things that I wanted to discover about the relationship between children and television. I used a variety of methodologies to research and find evidence (from primary and secondary sources). I first engaged in primary research and then used secondary sources to prove or disprove what I had found.

My first objective was to investigate advertising: whether children respond to adverts and what impact this has on them. In order to do this I took an ethnographical approach, which meant monitoring the viewing habits of two females: one aged 7 and one aged 4. I understand that ethnographical approaches are debatable, but I found this method useful within my study.

I began by looking at whether the attention of my two subjects altered when the adverts came on. I also looked at the effect of programmes which had 'embedded' adverts. *Blue Peter*, I was surprised to find, was one such programme. The editions of the programme broadcast around the Christmas period included reference to and review of many new products. I looked at whether my two subjects responded to these references in a way which was different to their response to normal adverts. Obviously, embedded advertising does not have the same visual and audio features as standard advertising and is much more subtle.

Children seem to learn a set of 'skills' in order to comprehend television and I looked at research conducted around format features in order to investigate this point. Research found that attention to content varies and is, to an extent, dependent upon the child's understanding of events occurring on television. I looked at a range of studies, including *Children and Television: the One-Eyed Monster?* by Barrie Gunter and Jill L. McAleer (2nd edn). In order to conduct my own investigation, I recorded a set of adverts (the Barbie Aeroplane, Meccano, Quavers and Bob the Builder) and looked at my subjects' responses to them. My findings matched those of academic studies in that I discovered that it was sound which most attracted the attention of the children and the visual element was a means to sustain this attention.

I wanted to find out what effect the visual element of an advert had on young children, and in particular what impact various characters had on their young audience. I asked one of the children what her favourite television character was and was surprised when she said Barbie (not so much a 'character' as a product familiar from adverts). I became very interested in whether or not blurring the boundaries

between television programmes and adverts was a marketing strategy used by companies. Research by Young (in *Ill Effects*) offered the theory that there was indeed confusion of meaning between these two very different kinds of television text.

My second objective was connected to the much-debated area of whether violence on television affects children — and if so, how they are affected. I wanted to study my two young subjects to find out whether they could distinguish between real and fictional representations of violence. David Buckingham has put forward the theory of the 'Electronic Child House'. Elizabeth Newson also discusses ideas about children's responses to violence on television and believes that exposure encourages children to commit violent acts. She puts forward a model in which children are passive consumers of what they see. I felt that these ideas needed to be put into a real context, so I devised a test. First, I logged the number of physically and verbally 'violent' acts portrayed on CITV within a 2-hour period, but found this research to be inconclusive because all I had done was total the acts and not study the impact of them on the child viewer. I then decided to monitor the viewing of my 7-year-old subject and record her answers to a series of questions. These questions were seemingly unconnected to the programme being viewed (*The X-Men*), e.g. 'What did you do at school today?', but the responses were significant. The first thing I noticed was the difficulty of gaining the child's attention when this programme was showing. My second observation was that the child was disobedient (not violent) after viewing. I have been very critical of the link between children's viewing and violent behaviour, but now believe that at the very least, the boundaries between right and wrong become more blurred.

In order to understand this area, I consulted a great deal of academic research from the book *Children and Television: the One-Eyed Monster?* mentioned above. I was particularly interested in the argument concerning intervening variables and feel that this placed the violence debate in a more 'human' context. The stimulus–response model, according to which children's behaviour is affected directly by what they absorb from television, was covered here and was highlighted in the book *Plug in Drug* in 1977. Systematic and scientific field studies have offered conclusions about violence too. Laboratory experiments like the Bobo Doll tests were also used to confirm a link between violent images and violent behaviour in children, but today these tests are deemed insubstantial and misleading.

The psychologist Michael Rich has stated that television affects children, but as a form of addiction. It is also argued that because children now often have a television set in their bedroom, the addictive quality of viewing is made even more prevalent because there is no one to censor either subject matter or length of viewing.

My final objective was to discover whether children learn from television. I spoke to my subjects' teachers and discovered that, on average, 7-year-olds watch no more than 2 hours of television per week in order to supplement their education and 4-year-olds watch around $1\frac{1}{2}$ hours. I discovered research which suggested that watching television helps to develop cognitive skills and that children appear to learn the ability to process and evaluate what they see. Durkin argues that 'genetic clues' are given showing that children start to build up 'media literacy' and learn to become better at processing and deciphering television messages, especially if this is part of a social process.

Children arguably make use of television to satisfy needs, either subconsciously (as a diversion) or actively (to pass time). This shows how powerful television is, but also indicates the fact that children are active producers of meaning and are a selective audience.

✏ The candidate begins well, outlining the aims and objectives of the project. The essay moves systematically through the various stages of research, offering a clear, focused and evaluative response.

(2) What were the conclusions you came to following your investigation of your topic?

■ ■ ■

From what I have discovered about children and television, I have developed the thesis that children adopt television because of the various roles it can play in their lives, especially advertising and learning. This suggests that television is a constructive medium for children, which is interesting because the opposite has often been said to be true. However, arguments that television has a negative role in the lives of children because it exposes them to violence have been challenged, especially by theorists such as David Buckingham. I feel that television plays a positive role for children in that they start to understand the nature of programmes and this develops with age. Academic research fits my hypothesis that children learn from television and that what they learn depends on the types of programme they watch, as well as on their ability to identify different programmes. Content is also an important factor. In cognitive development, children should respond to meanings as well as physical happenings. This, of course, is a hypothetical idea and can be challenged.

Researchers such as Young found that children's attention to television programmes varies with content and that format constitutes an important influence. Combined with David Buckingham's idea that television is a teacher, there is a strong argument that television has a fundamental role in children's education. From what I observed of my two subjects, programmes like *The Tweenies* helped the children to learn nursery rhymes, morals and interpersonal skills.

From my research I have deduced that gender roles are also informed by the programmes children watch. The parents of my two subjects identified the programme *Rugrats* as an influential factor in how their children behave. They said that the programme offered quite traditional gender roles within its characterisation and that the children had begun playing 'mums and dads' after watching it. However, from my study of the programme, I noted that the gender roles portrayed were not quite so fixed. There is a high-powered female executive within the programme, who seems at odds with the parents' analysis.

Adverts play a role in children's lives and are significant in influencing them. Research on adverts (such as that of Young) challenges the view that children are passive and instead puts forward the idea that children develop a working knowledge of advertising techniques (music, persuasion through voices and child models). We can therefore conclude that media literacy helps children to identify what to believe and what to ignore.

One of my subjects found the real-life events on the news very unnerving and worrying, so television does have an informative function and ensures that news reaches children as well as adults. My subject was also concerned by cartoons, such as *Tom and Jerry*, where the characters seem to be indestructible. This puts reality and fantasy distinctions under the microscope and a lack of realism is now becoming more noticeable in older children. Physical features such as animation and costume help children to identify images as 'unreal'.

From my research, I have concluded that children are active viewers of television. I am still wary of violence debates and have yet to find any concrete evidence to support my findings (which are already inconclusive). The 'uses and gratifications' model argues that children use television to meet a variety of needs and I would add that it performs a number of different roles in their lives. Children get a great deal out of television by being selective and using it for their own purposes. For example, they may watch television in order to be entertained or to be informed. The purpose served by watching television changes constantly, depending on the type of programme, and will also vary with age. Children develop the ability to see meanings within programmes, and can begin to see the function of adverts (to sell things) from an early age. This means that television performs a dual function. It both translates and constructs ideologies for the child viewer. The child viewer is therefore able to comprehend ideology and be receptive to its influence at the same time.

This answer evaluates primary and secondary sources and challenges their validity where necessary. It is a discriminating response. Examples are used in an appropriate way and it is clear that the candidate has used thorough research to reach informed conclusions.

Overall, this is an excellent response. The candidate refers confidently to a wide range of primary and secondary sources, using them in an appropriate manner. Both answers exhibit a high level of research and evaluation, and would be awarded a grade A.

Sport and the media

(1) Describe and discuss the research methodologies you used to investigate your question.

■ ■ ■

Grade-C answer

Today sport and the media go hand in hand. They have had a long and difficult relationship. I decided to focus on football, because it has always proved very lucrative for broadcasters. To investigate this I decided to look into the battle for television rights and ratings between ITV, BBC and Sky. I decided to investigate this globally.

My first research area was the relationship between producers, institutions and the industry involved. I attempted primary research by e-mailing two key men, the BBC head of sport, Peter Salmon, and the controller of ITV sport, Brian Barwick. Unfortunately, neither replied. I had many potential avenues for secondary research, the first of which was newspaper cuttings from the *Sun*, the *Mirror*, the *Times* and the *Guardian* newspapers. During my research period, three major stories dominated the news: the auctioning of premiership television rights, the poor ratings for ITV's *The Premiership* programme and the demise of the ITV sports channel and its effects on the football league.

I used the internet too. I was able to carry out an extensive search for articles covering the issues, dating as far back as 1999. I also used class notes I had made on the Broadcasting Acts of 1990 and 1996 in connection with legislation on media ownership and retention of major sporting events for television, and watched an edition of *Panorama* which investigated the relationship between football and the media.

I visited my local library to find information, as well as my college library and the central library in Birmingham. The following books were helpful to me: *The Business of Football* by Michie and Oughton, *Moving the Goalposts: Football's Exploitation* by Horton, *Sport and Society* by Jay J. Coakley and *The Television Handbook* by Patricia Holland. Popular criticism of football is not hard to find. I read the *Sun* and the *Mirror* tabloids, as well as the *Guardian* broadsheet. To gain a fan's perspective I regularly visited **www.fromtheterrace.co.uk**. The radio was a good source of information too. Shows like Radio 5 Live's *606* were useful sources.

The majority of primary research I conducted came under the heading of 'audience reception'. I created a questionnaire and asked a mixed-gender group questions such as, 'Which sports programme do you watch?' and 'Which is your favourite medium for consuming sports?' I felt it was important to find out the opinions of people my age and conducted a focus group with a sample of 17–18-year-olds. All of the participants in the focus group were male. While I recognise that there is a growing number of women who enjoy football, it is generally accepted that men know more about football than women. Besides, I didn't know any women I could include in my group.

topic

I used both primary and secondary sources for my research and utilised a whole range of resources.

> 📝 The research is rather unfocused, and although the essay contains some reflection on research methodology, this should have been sustained throughout the response.

(2) What were the conclusions you came to following your investigation of your topic?

■ ■ ■

The relationship between media conglomerates and sports agencies has, on the whole, been smooth — that is, until the twenty-first century. Football is big business. Ever since the creation of the Football Association premier league in the early 1990s, media companies have sought a slice of the action. The premier league sells its exclusive television rights for hundreds of millions of pounds. It has made Sky extremely successful.

In the early 1990s, satellite broadcasting was struggling. There was a distinct lack of subscribers. However, Sky acquired the exclusive rights to live premiership football. This not only saved the broadcasting company, but built it up into such a lucrative enterprise that it became impossible for anyone else to challenge for the live rights. Sky can now outbid all other broadcasters for the rights to football matches.

The premier league now offers four packages to television companies. At the last auction, these packages brought in over £1 billion. To attempt to influence the sales, television companies have sought to buy into top football clubs. NTL, Sky, Carlton and Granada have all bought shares in top clubs. Sky even tried to buy Manchester United, but this was eventually rejected by the Monopolies and Mergers Commission. Sporting agencies seem to be relinquishing control to broadcasters in the pursuit of money. There are now 12 possible kick-off times for football matches in this country. The traditional time of 3 p.m. on a Saturday is disappearing fast. In 2001, the UEFA cup semifinal between Liverpool and Barcelona, in Spain, was put back 15 minutes so that the BBC could show an extended episode of the flagship soap *EastEnders*.

Another way in which the media have influenced the game is through the attraction and retention of audiences. Sky has no less than 10 channels on which football is shown and the internet contains thousands of dedicated websites. Ideologically, the media has developed sport into a global phenomenon. In recent years there has been cultural imperialism of the Far East, not least due to football. Sky's principal shareholder, News International, controls satellite broadcasting in Asia and America too. The 2002 World Cup, hosted by Japan and South Korea, saw a huge amount of home support for the English national team, possibly even more support than from its own country.

The media domination of sport has led to an increase in the popularity of some sports, such as football, but a distinct lack of coverage of minority sports such as golf, snooker and bowls. These are squashed into programmes like the BBC's *Grandstand*.

New technology has stimulated an increased interest in the game as well as causing new problems. Interactivity brings the viewer closer to the action than ever before, negating the need to actually attend games. The in-depth analysis of more camera angles and replays adds to the pressure on players and officials to make the right decisions. Wrong decisions can be scrutinised closely.

The media have developed football into an advertiser's dream. Sponsors can become involved with clubs, kit, players, competitions and television programmes. Players are now major celebrities and make more money from off-field activities than on-field activities. For the clubs, the money they receive is vital. It enables them to pay the best players huge wages. Clubs are now in a state of financial crisis. As the money dries up, ordinary fans are hit hardest. It is the fans who buy the tickets, shirts, television subscriptions and player-backed products. The media have taken the game away from normal fans. It is no longer the 'working man's game'. Neither media conglomerates nor their sporting counterparts listen to fans any longer. They are consumed by greed, which is already threatening the survival of lower-league clubs and could have damaged the national game. The media's domination of the development of sport has in my opinion been to the detriment of supporters and the sporting ideals on which these games were based.

e The candidate attempts to relate the evidence collected to the wider topic, but this is not sustained. The answer should have been clearer and more systematic in its argument.

_e_ Although there are plenty of useful references to sources and resources in both of these answers, the candidate does not evaluate these fully. Without thorough evaluation and a focused argument, this answer would not gain more than a grade C.